HAL·LEONARD®
HARMONICA PLAY-ALONG
AUDIO ACCESS INCLUDED

VOL. 3
BLUES ROCK

T0087639

Harmonica by Clint Hoover

PLAYBACK+
Speed • Pitch • Balance • Loop

To access audio visit:
www.halleonard.com/mylibrary

Enter Code
1137-4275-2768-7012

ISBN 978-1-4234-2347-8

Visit Hal Leonard Online at
www.halleonard.com

Contact us:
Hal Leonard
7777 West Bluemound Road
Milwaukee, WI 53213
Email: info@halleonard.com

In Europe, contact:
Hal Leonard Europe Limited
42 Wigmore Street
Marylebone, London, W1U 2RN
Email: info@halleonardeurope.com

In Australia, contact:
Hal Leonard Australia Pty. Ltd.
4 Lentara Court
Cheltenham, Victoria, 3192 Australia
Email: info@halleonard.com.au

HARMONICA NOTATION LEGEND

Harmonica music can be notated two different ways: on a *musical staff*, and in *tablature*.

THE MUSICAL STAFF shows pitches and rhythms and is divided by bar lines into measures. Pitches are named after the first seven letters of the alphabet.

TABLATURE graphically represents the harmonica music. Each note will be accompanied by a number, 1 through 10, indicating what hole you are to play. The arrow that follows indicates whether to blow or draw. (All examples are shown using a C diatonic harmonica.)

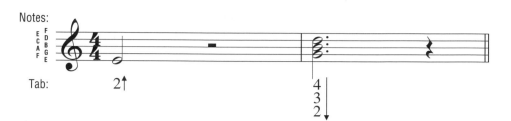

Blow (exhale) into 2nd hole.

Draw (inhale) 2nd, 3rd, & 4th holes together.

Notes on the C Harmonica

Exhaled (Blown) Notes

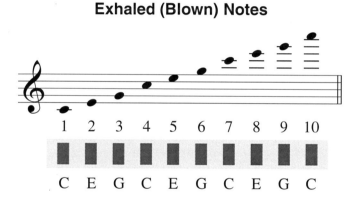

Inhaled (Drawn) Notes

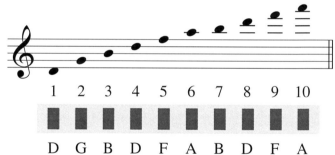

Bends

Blow Bends

- 1/4 step
- 1/2 step
- 1 step
- 1 1/2 steps

Draw Bends

- 1/4 step
- 1/2 step
- 1 step
- 1 1/2 steps

Definitions for Special Harmonica Notation

SLURRED BEND: Play (draw) 3rd hole, then bend the note down one whole step.

3↓   3↗

GRACE NOTE BEND: Starting with a pre-bent note, immediately release bend to the target note.

2↗ 2↓

VIBRATO: Begin adding vibrato to the sustained note on beat 3.

4↑   (4↑)

TONGUE BLOCKING: Using your tongue to block holes 2 & 3, play octaves on holes 1 & 4.

4↑
1

NOTE: Tablature numbers in parentheses are used when:

- The note is sustained, but a new articulation begins (such as vibrato), or
- The quantity of notes being sustained changes, or
- A change in dynamics (volume) occurs.

Additional Musical Definitions

D.S. al Coda

- Go back to the sign (𝄋), then play until the measure marked "***To Coda***," then skip to the section labelled "**Coda**."

D.C. al Fine

- Go back to the beginning of the song and play until the measure marked "***Fine***" (end).

- Repeat measures between signs.

(accent)

- Accentuate the note (play initial attack louder).

(staccato)

- Play the note short.

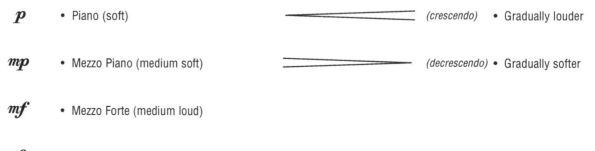

- When a repeated section has different endings, play the first ending only the first time and the second ending only the second time.

Dynamics

p   • Piano (soft)

mp   • Mezzo Piano (medium soft)

mf   • Mezzo Forte (medium loud)

f   • Forte (loud)

(crescendo) • Gradually louder

(decrescendo) • Gradually softer

Big Ten Inch Record

Words and Music by Fred Weismantel

HARMONICA
Player: Steven Tyler
Harp Key: D Diatonic

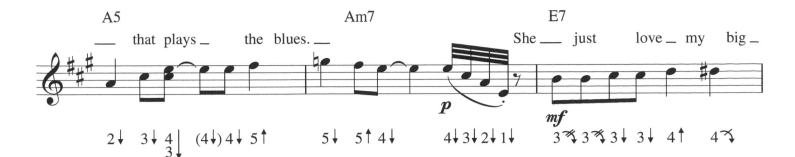

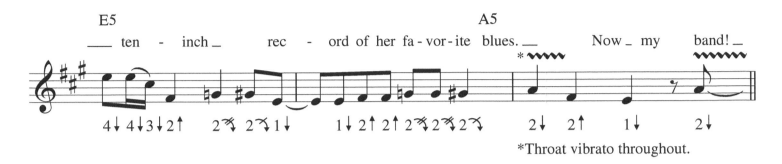

*Throat vibrato throughout.

Guitar Solo

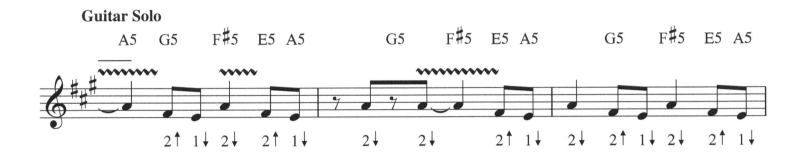

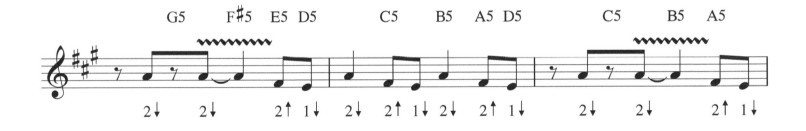

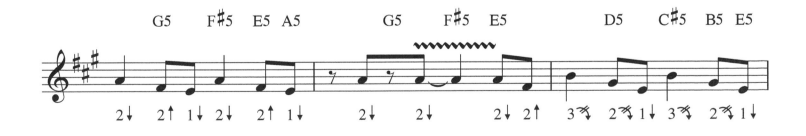

Verse

D5
___ night I tried to tease ___ her;   I gave my love a lit - tle pinch. ___

1↑   2↑   2↓   3↗   3↗   3↗   3↑ 3↑ 2↑ 2↑   2↓ 2↓ 3↓ 3↓ 4↓ 4↓ 5↑

C#5   D5
___ But she said, "Now stop the jiv - in',   'n' now

5↓ 5↓ 5↑ 4↓   4↓   1↑   2↑   2↑ 2↓   3↗3↓   3↗3↓   3↗   3↑   2↑ 2↑
                                        2↓   2↓

Chorus

E5   N.C.   C#5   D5
whip out your big ten - inch ___ rec - ord of a band that plays the blues, ___

1↓   2↓ 1↑ 2↑   2↓ 3↗ 2↓

D9   G#5   A5   Am7
___ well, a band ___ that plays ___ the blues." ___   She ___

3↗ 2↓ 3↗ 2↓   3↑ 3↑ 2↑ 2↑   2↓ 2↓ 3↓ 3↓   4↓ 4↓ 5↑   5↓ 5↓ 5↑ 4↓
        1↓

E7   E5
___ just loves ___ my big ___ ten - inch ___ rec -

3↗ 3↗ 3↓ 3↓ 4↑   4↗ 4↓   4↗ 3↓ 2↓ 2↑ 2↑ 2↗ 2↗ 2↗ 1↓

Verse

A5   D5
- ord of her fa - vor - ite blues. ___ 3. I, I, I'll ___ cov - er her with ___ kiss-

1↓ 2↑ 2↑ 2↗ 2↗ 2↗   2↓ 2↑   1↓ 2↓   1↑ 1↑ 2↑ 2↑ 1↓ 2↓ 2↑ 3↗

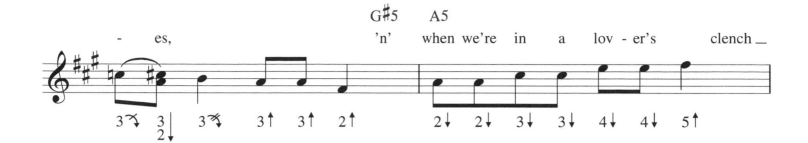

G#5　A5

- es,　'n' when we're in a lov - er's clench

C#5　D5

she ___ gets all ex - cit -

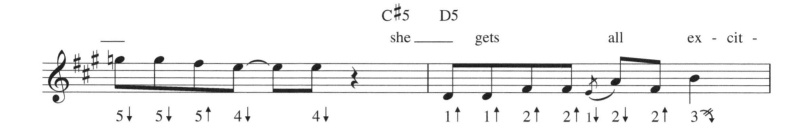

E5　N.C.　　　　　　　　　　C#5

- ed.　When she beg for my big ten - inch ___ rec - ord of a

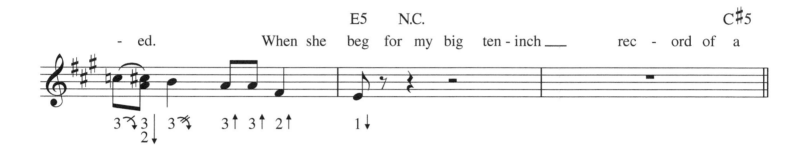

Chorus

D5　　　　　　　　　D9　　　　G#5　A5

band that plays ___ the blues, ___　well, a band ___ that plays ___ the blues. ___

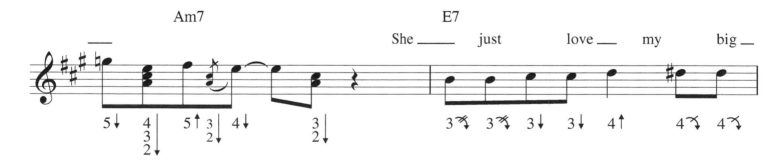

Am7　　　　　　　　　　　E7

She ___ just love ___ my big ___

E5　　　　　　　　　　　　　　　　A5

___ ten - inch ___ rec - ord of her fa - vor - ite blues. ___

Chorus

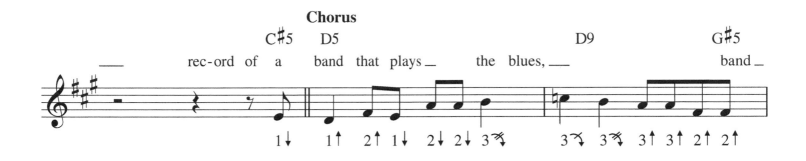

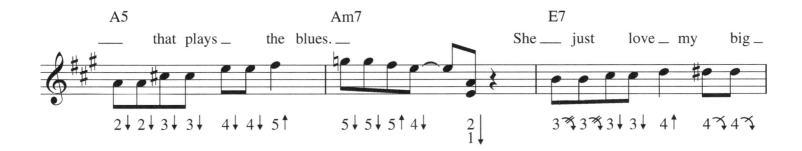

Outro

*Played as even eighth-notes.

On the Road Again

Words and Music by Alan Wilson and Floyd Jones

HARMONICA
Player: Alan Wilson
Harp Key: A Diatonic

G5 A5

*- ⌐

3⤵   2↓   4↑   4↓   5↓   6↑   7⤵   6↑ 5↓ 4↓ 4⤵ 4↑

*Played as even eighth-notes.

E5

3⤵ 2↓ 2⤵ 1↓ 1⤵ 1↓ 2⤵2↓ 2⤵1↓ 2⤵2↓ 2⤵1↓ 2⤵2↓ 2⤵1↓ 2⤵

G5 A5   E5

4. Take   a

2↓ 2⤵1↓ 2⤵2↓ 2⤵1↓ 1⤵1↓ 2⤵   2↓   2↓   2↑

**As before.

Verse

E5   G5   A5

hint from me, mom-ma, _ please ___ don't you cry _ no _ more. _   Don't you cry   no

2↓   2↓ 2↓   2↓   2↓ 2↓   2↓   2↓ 2↓   2↓ 3⤵ 4↑ 5↓4↓3↓

E5

more.   Take   a   hint from me, mom-ma, _   please _   don't you cry ___ no more. _

2↓   2↓2↓   2↓   2↓   2↓   2↓   2↓   2↓   2↑   2⤵ 2↓ 2⤵1↓   2↑
                                                      1   1

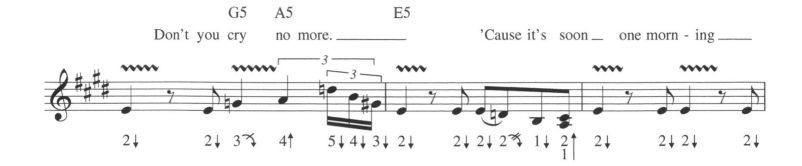

Verse

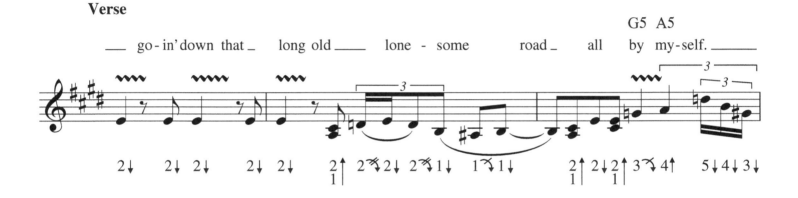

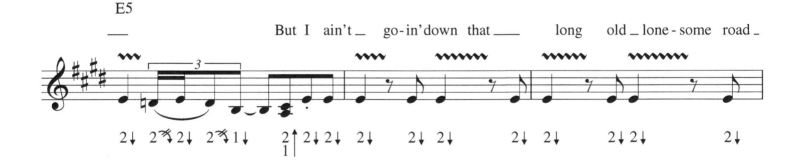

car-ry some - bod   -   y else. _

Outro-Harmonica Solo

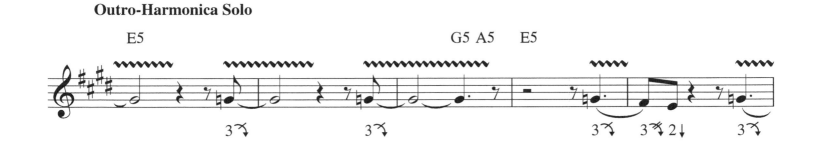

Begin fade

*All except sitar.

Fade out

(Sitar)   (Guitar)

Roadhouse Blues

Words and Music by The Doors

H A R M O N I C A
Player: John Sebastian
Harp Key: A Diatonic

Verse

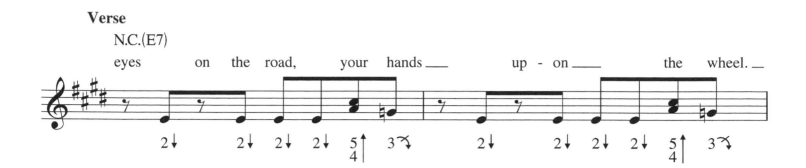

*Throat vibrato throughout

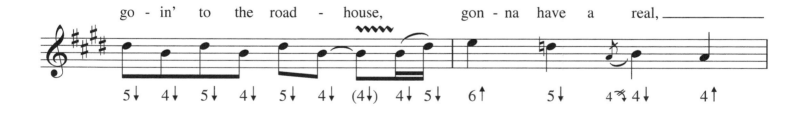

Interlude

E7

2↓ 2↓ 2↓ 5↑ 3↘ 2↓ 2↓ 2↓ 5↑ 3↘
        4↑   4↑

2. Yeah,   in

2↓ 2↓ 2↓ 2↓ 5↑ 3↘ 2↓ 2↓ 2↓ 5↑ 3↘
            4↑   4↑

Verse

E7

back   of the road - house they got   some _ bun - ga - lows. _

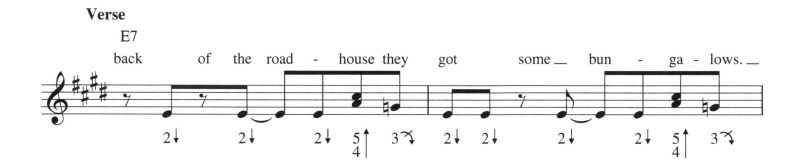

2↓ 2↓ 2↓ 5↑ 3↘ 2↓ 2↓ 2↓ 2↓ 5↑ 3↘
        4↑   4↑

Yeah,   in

2↓ 3↓ 4↑ 4↘4↓ 4↘4↓ 5↓ 4↓ 4↘4↓ 4↘3↓2↓ 3↘ 2↓ 2↘ 2↓ (2↓) 2↓

back   of the road - house they got   some _ bun - ga - lows. _

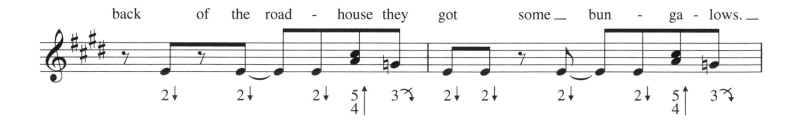

2↓ 2↓ 2↓ 5↑ 3↘ 2↓ 2↓ 2↓ 2↓ 5↑ 3↘
        4↑   4↑

And

2↓ 2↓ 3↓ 4↑ 4↘4↓ 4↘4↓ 4↘3↓ 2↓ 3↘ 2↓ 2↘ 2↓ (2↓)   4↓

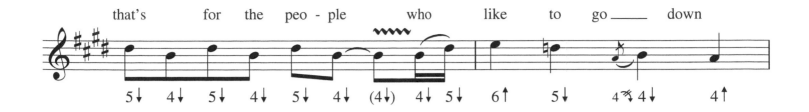

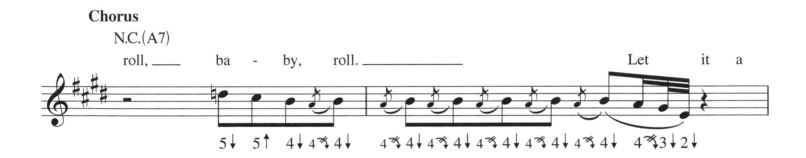

Chorus

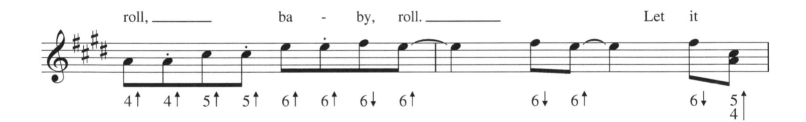

Guitar Solo

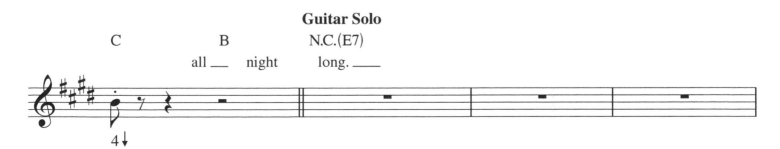

Interlude

N.C.(E7)

You got - ta   roll,   roll,   roll, you got - ta

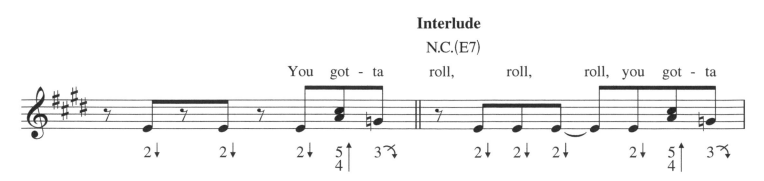

thrill _ my soul, al - right.

Roll, roll, roll, roll a through my soul __ *de got ta

*Nonsense syllables

peep - a con - cha choo - chom, paw conk conk, __ ka - don - ta

hay - cha coon - a may - cha, ba, ba loo la hey chow, __

__ bow pa key chow ee - sown comp, __ yeah, _____

*Played as even eighth-notes.

Harmonica Solo

N.C.(E7)

right. ____

21

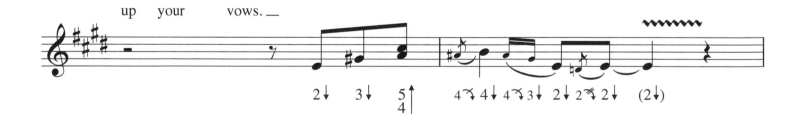

right now.

4↷ 4↓ 4↑ 3↓ 2↓ (2↓)   2↓ 2↓ 2↓ 5↑ 3↷   2↓ 2↓ 2↓ 5↑ 3↷
                                    4   4

E7

3. When I

2↓ 2↓ 2↓ 5↑ 3↷ 2↓ 2↓ 2↓ 5↑ 3↷
              4   4

Verse

E7

woke up this morn - in' I got ___ my - self a beer. ___

2↓ 2↓ 2↓ 5↑ 3↷ 2↓ 2↓ 2↓ 5↑ 3↷
              4   4

___

When I

2↓ 3↓ 4↑ 4↷ 4↓ 4↓ 3↓ 2↓ 3↷ 2↓ 2↷ 2↓ (2↓)

woke up this morn - in' ___ I got my - self a beer. ___

2↓ 2↓ 2↓ 5↑ 3↷ 2↓ 2↓ 2↓ 2↓ 5↑ 3↷
              4   4

___

The

2↓ 2↓ 3↓ 5↑ 4↷ 4↓ 4↷ 4↓ 4↷ 3↓ 2↓ 3↷ 2↓ 2↷ 2↓ (2↓) 4↓
              4

23

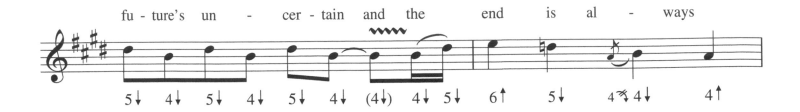

Outro-Chorus

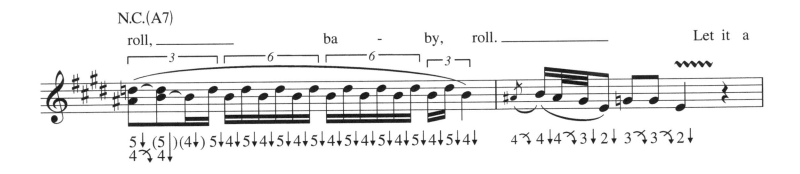

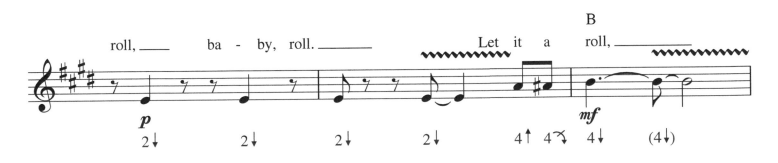

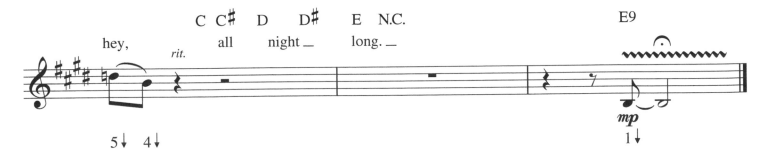

Waitin' for the Bus

Words and Music by Billy F Gibbons and Dusty Hill

H A R M O N I C A
Player: Billy Gibbons
Harp Key: D Diatonic

Intro
Moderate Blues ♩ = 100

N.C. A7

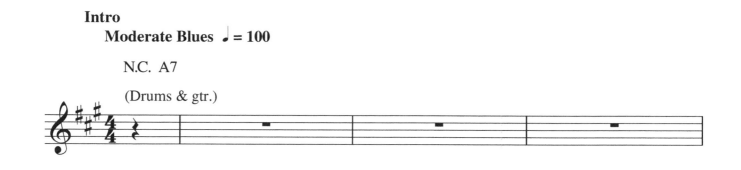

1. Have mer -

Verse
A7

- cy; been wait-in' for the bus all day.

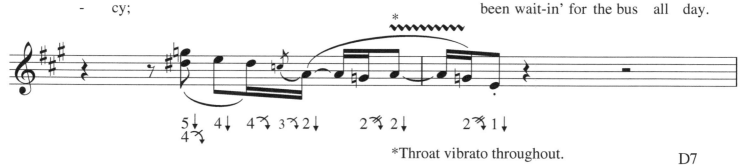

*Throat vibrato throughout.

D7

Have mer -

- cy; been wait-in' for the bus all day.

A7

*1 1/2 step bend.

Verse

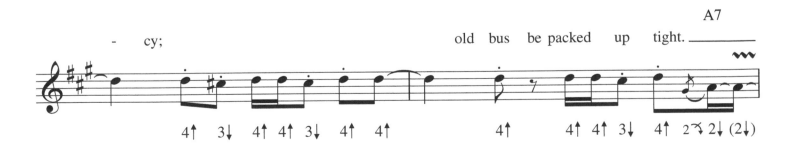

26

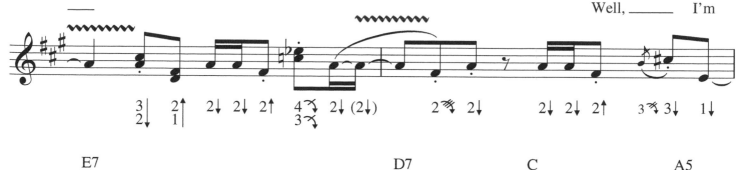

Well, _____ I'm

E7   D7   C   A5

glad   just   to   get   on   and   home   to - night.

Harmonica Solo

D5   E5   A7

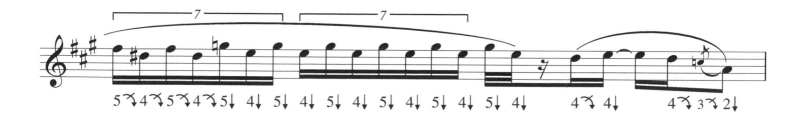

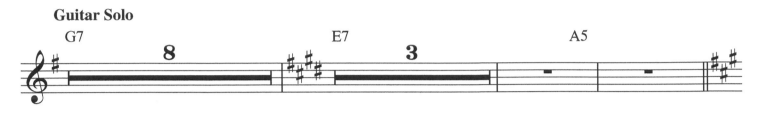

Guitar Solo

Interlude

A7

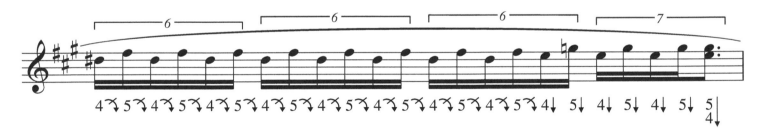

Verse

A7

3. Right   on; _____

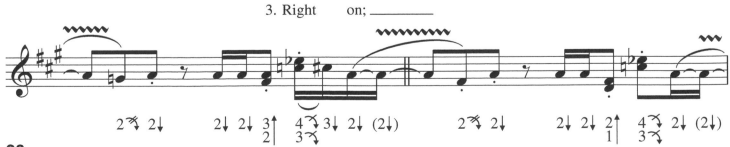

that bus done got me back.

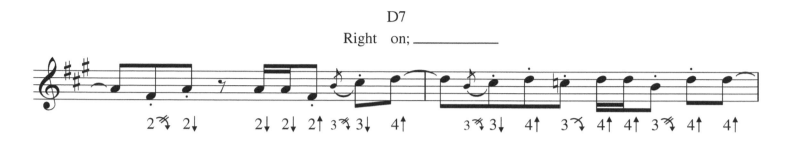

2↗ 2↓ 2↓ 2↓ 2↑ 3↘ 2↓ (2↓) 2↗ 2↓ 2↓ 2↓ 2↑ 3↓ 2↓

D7
Right on; _____

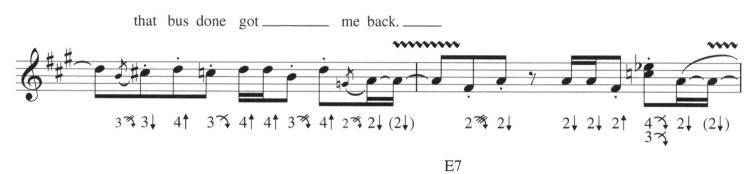

2↗ 2↓ 2↓ 2↓ 2↑ 3↘ 3↓ 4↑ 3↘ 3↓ 4↑ 3↘ 4↑ 4↑ 3↘ 4↑ 4↑

A7
that bus done got _____ me back. _____

3↘ 3↓ 4↑ 3↘ 4↑ 4↑ 3↘ 4↑ 2↗ 2↓ (2↓) 2↗ 2↓ 2↓ 2↓ 2↑ 4↘ 2↓ (2↓)
                                                         3↘

E7
Well, I'll be rid - in' on that bus till I

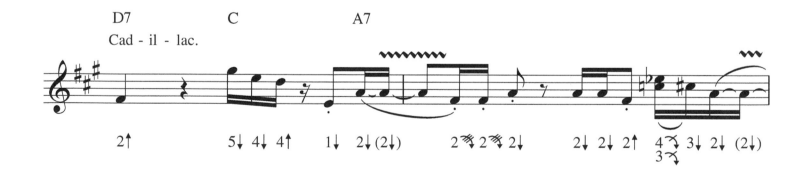

2↗ 2↓ 2↓ 2↓ 2↑ 3↘ 3↓ 1↓ 2↗ 2↘ 4↑

D7   C   A7
Cad - il - lac.

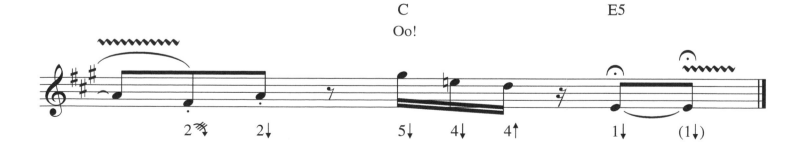

2↑ 5↓ 4↓ 4↑ 1↓ 2↓ (2↓) 2↗ 2↘ 2↓ 2↓ 2↓ 2↑ 4↘ 3↓ 2↓ (2↓)
                                                3↘

C   E5
Oo!

2↗ 2↓ 5↓ 4↓ 4↑ 1↓ (1↓)

Rollin' and Tumblin'

Written by McKinley Morganfield (Muddy Waters)

H A R M O N I C A
Player: Jack Bruce
Harp Key: D Diatonic

Chorus

*Throat vibrato throughout unless otherwise indicated.

D
Hey, ___ hey, hey, ___

C   G
hey, ___ hey, hey. ___

1. We were

Verse
C
roll - ing and tumb - lin', I cried the whole night long. ___

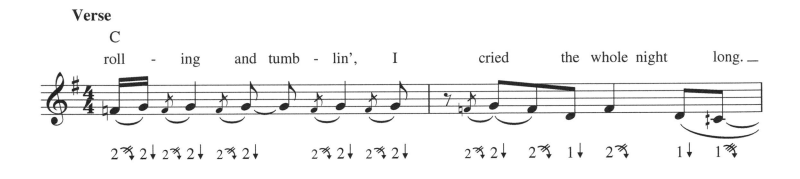

G

We were

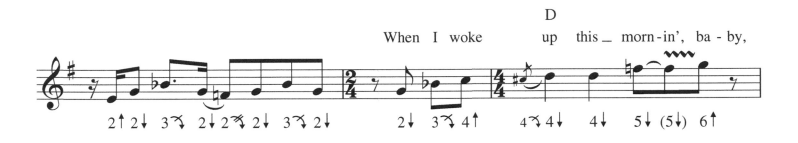

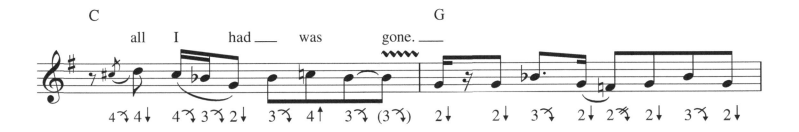

Verse

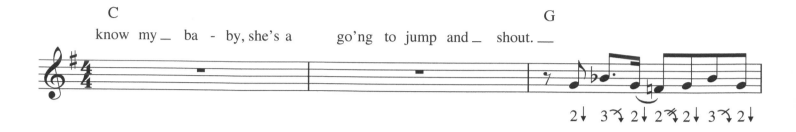

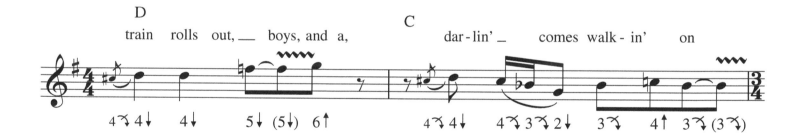

Harmonica Solo

G

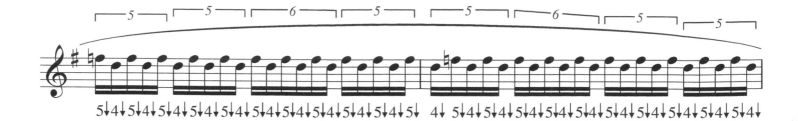

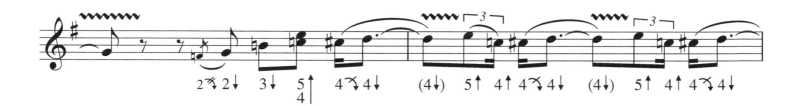

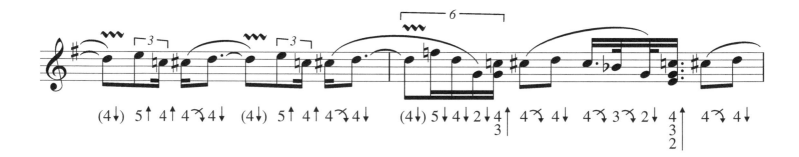

*Hand vibrato

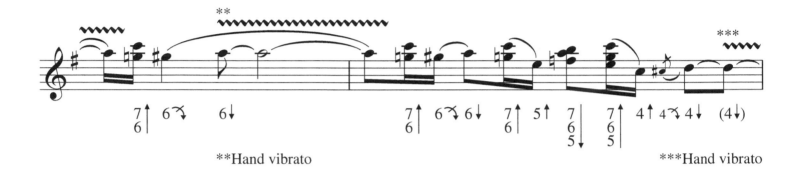

**Hand vibrato

***Hand vibrato

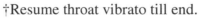

†Resume throat vibrato till end.

Interlude

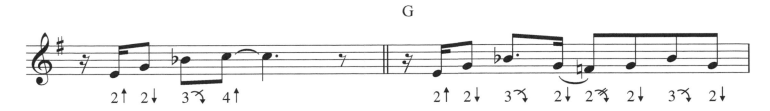

Chorus

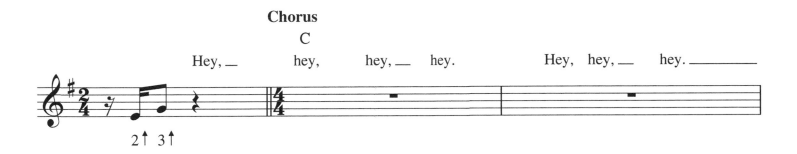

Hey, —

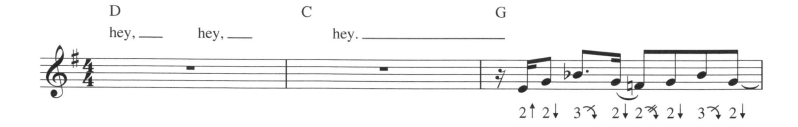

D   C   G

hey, ___   hey, ___   hey. _____

Verse

C

3. Well, the   five - man   whis -   tle,   now,

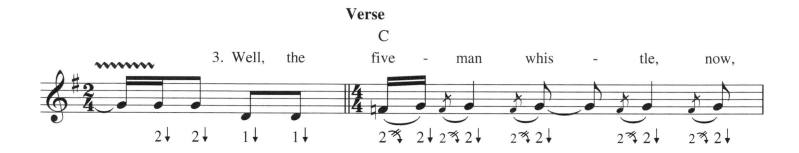

G

fire - man rings   the   bell. ____

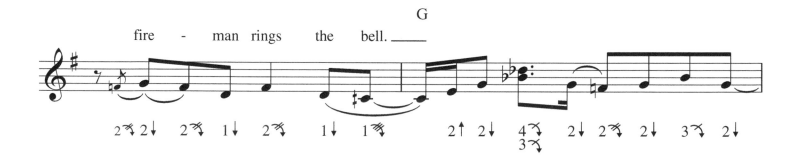

40

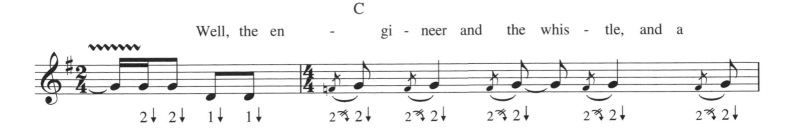

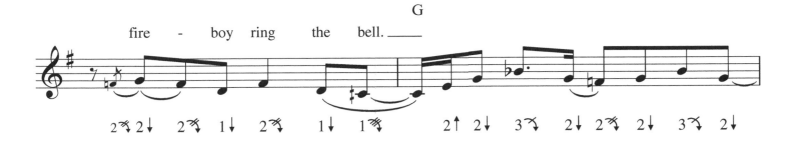

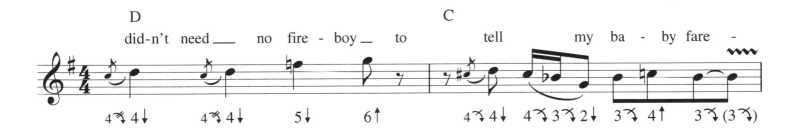

Train Kept A-Rollin'

**Words and Music by Tiny Bradshaw,
Lois Mann and Howie Kay**

HARMONICA
Player: Keith Relf
Harp Key: A Diatonic

42

*Throat vibrato throughout.

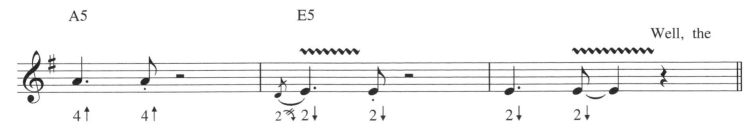

Interlude

*3/4 step bend

Guitar Solo

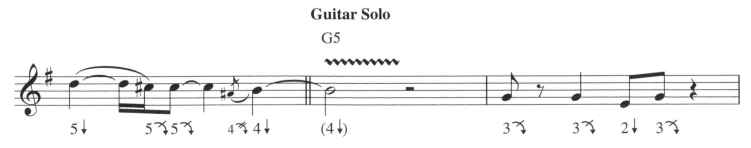

A5

G5

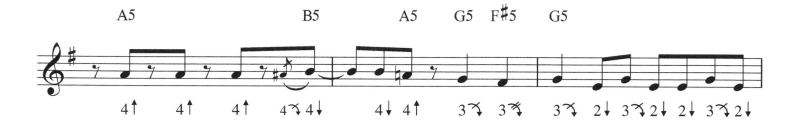

A5   B5   A5   G5   F#5   G5

A5

G5

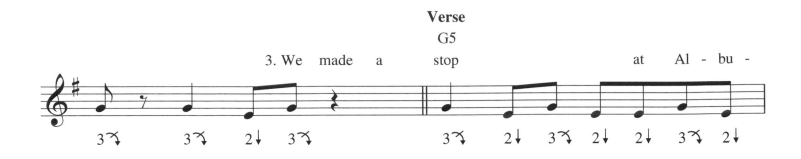

Verse

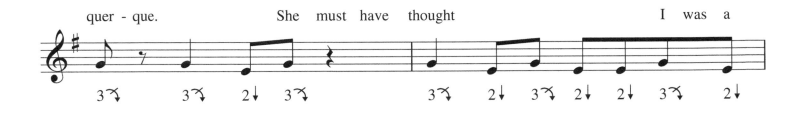

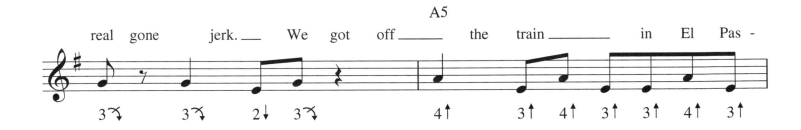

G5

Well,   the

Coda

Outro
E5

N.C.

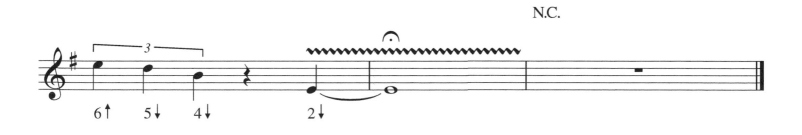

Additional Lyrics

2. Get along,
   Sweet little woman, get along, be on your way.
   Get along,
   Sweet little woman, get along, be on your way,
   With a heave and a ho, ah, well, I just couldn't let her go.

Train, Train

Words and Music by Shorty Medlocke

HARMONICA
Players: Cub Koda & Shorty Medlocke
Harp Keys: G & A Diatonic

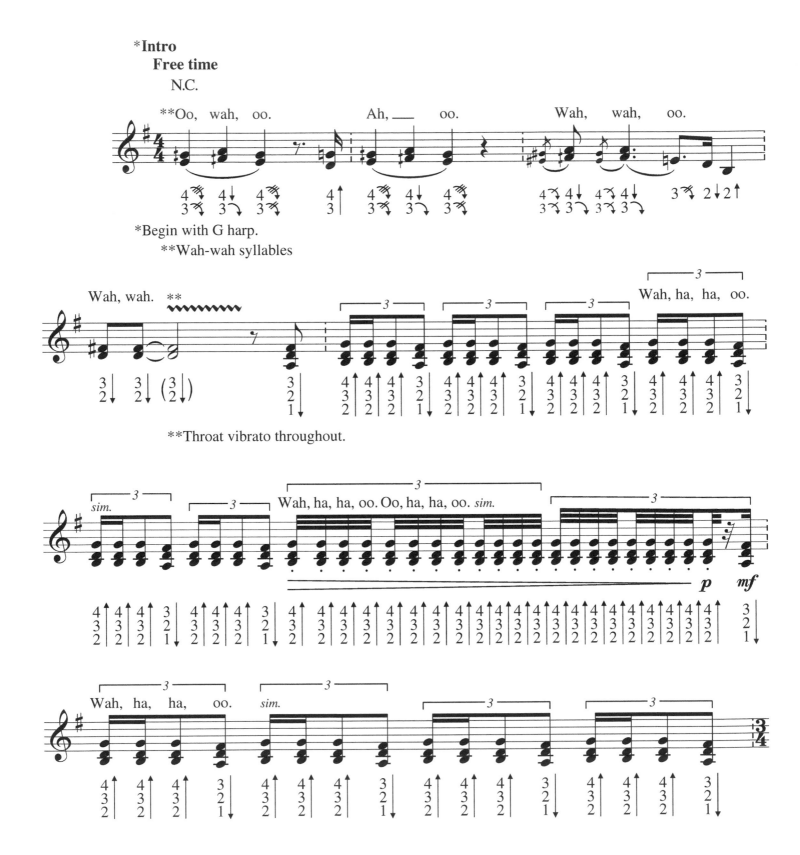

*Begin with G harp.

**Wah-wah syllables

**Throat vibrato throughout.

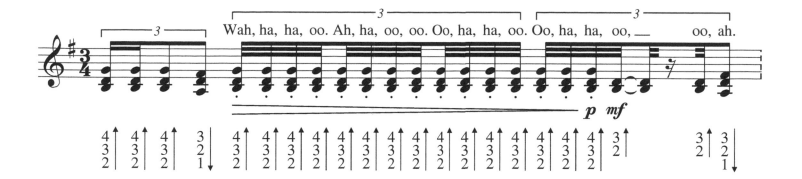

Wah, ha, ha, oo. Ah, ha, oo, oo. Oo, ha, ha, oo. Oo, ha, ha, oo, __ oo, ah.

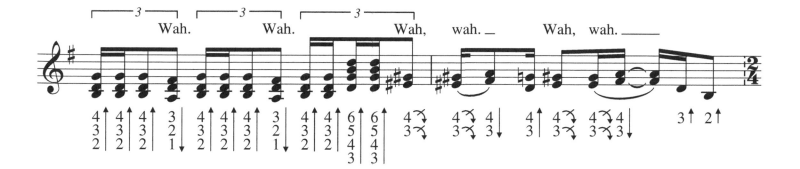

Wah. Wah. Wah, wah. __ Wah, wah. ___

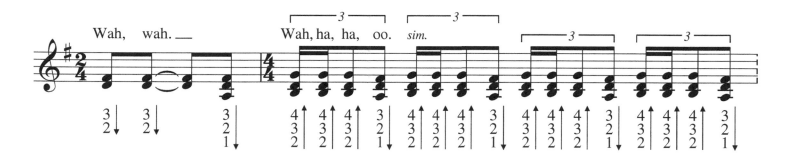

Wah, wah. __ Wah, ha, ha, oo. sim.

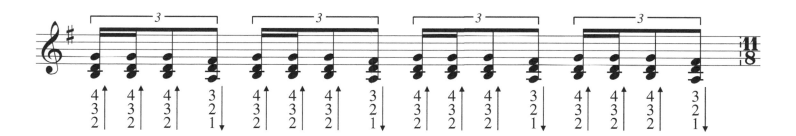

Wah, ha, oo. Wah, ha, oo. sim.

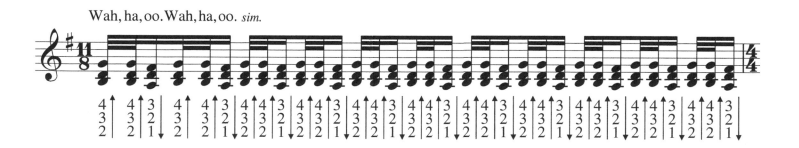

Moderate Rock ♩ = 122

E5

*

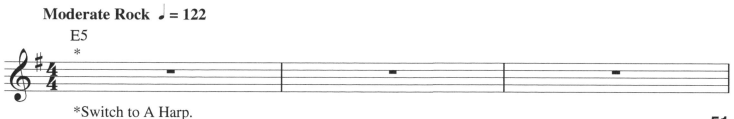

*Switch to A Harp.

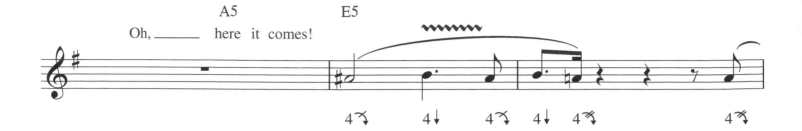

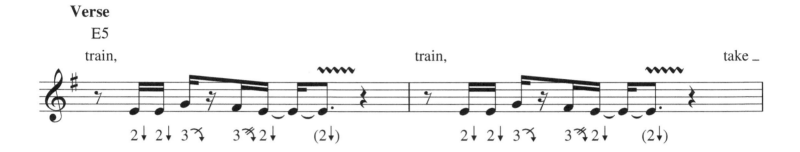

Verse

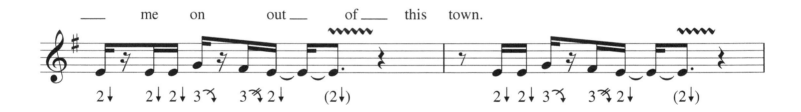

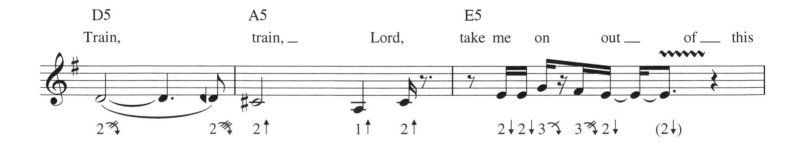

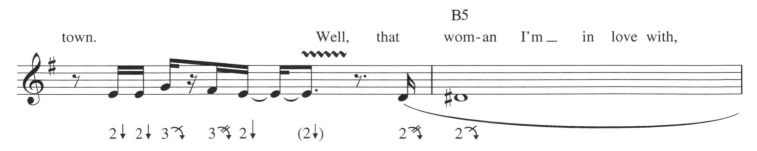

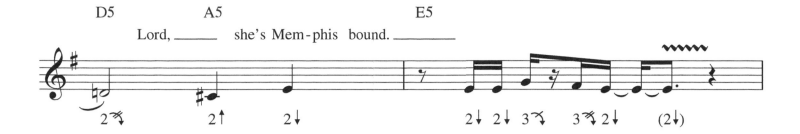

D5　　　　　A5　　　　　　　　　　E5

Lord, _____ she's Mem-phis bound. _____

2↯　　2↑　　2↓　　　　　2↓ 2↓ 3↯　3↯ 2↓　(2↓)

Verse

E5

2. Well,　　　leav　　　　　　　-　　　　　in'

4↑　　　　　2↓ 3↯　3↯ 2↓　(2↓)

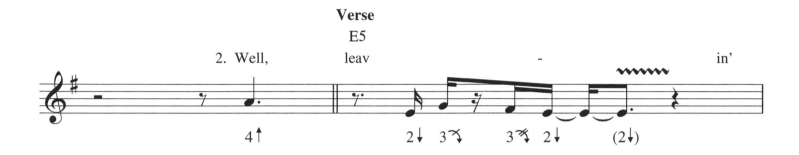

here,　　　　I'm just a　rag　-　ged-y _____　ho - bo. __

2↓ 2↓ 3↯　3↯ 2↓　(2↓)　　　2↓ 2↓ 3↯　3↯ 2↓　(2↓)

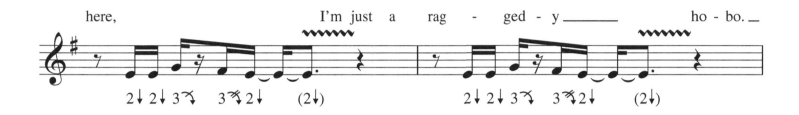

　　　　　　　　　　D5　　　　　　A5

__　　　　　Lord, I'm leav　-　in'　here, __　　I'm just a

2↓ 2↓ 3↯　3↯ 2↓　(2↓)　　　2↯　　　2↓ 2↯　2↑

E5

rag　-　ged-y _____　ho - bo. _____　　　　Well, that

2↓ 2↓ 3↯　3↯ 2↓　(2↓)　　　2↓ 2↓ 3↯　3↯ 2↓　(2↓)

B5　　　　　　　　　　　　　　　　　D5　　　　　A5

wom-an I'm __　in　love with,　　　Lord, _____　she's got to go. __

2↯ 2↯　　　　　　　　　　　　　2↯　　2↑　　2↓

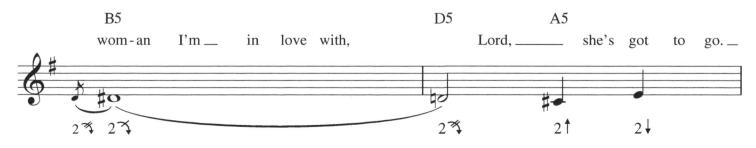

Guitar Solo

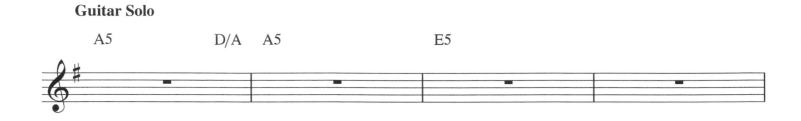

Harmonica Solo

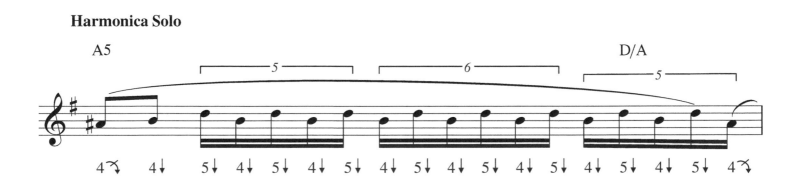

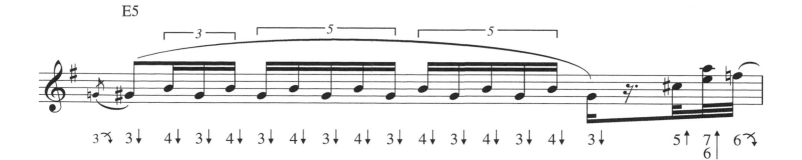

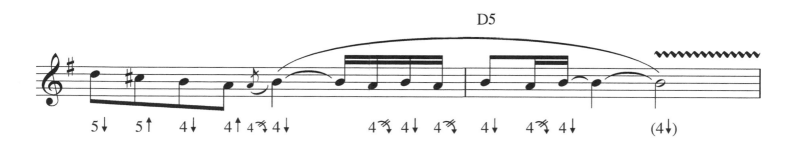

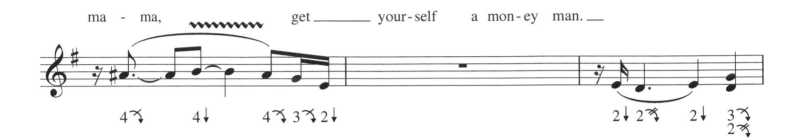

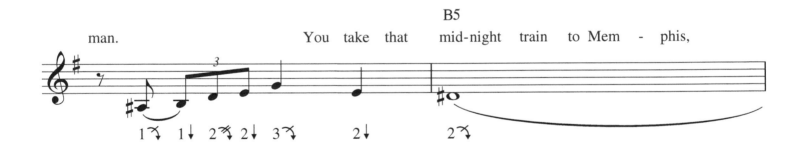

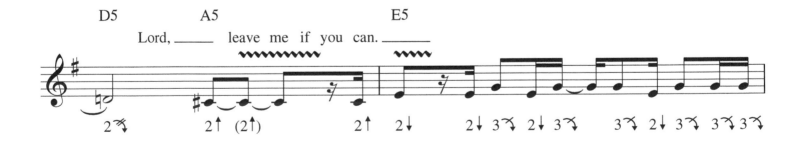

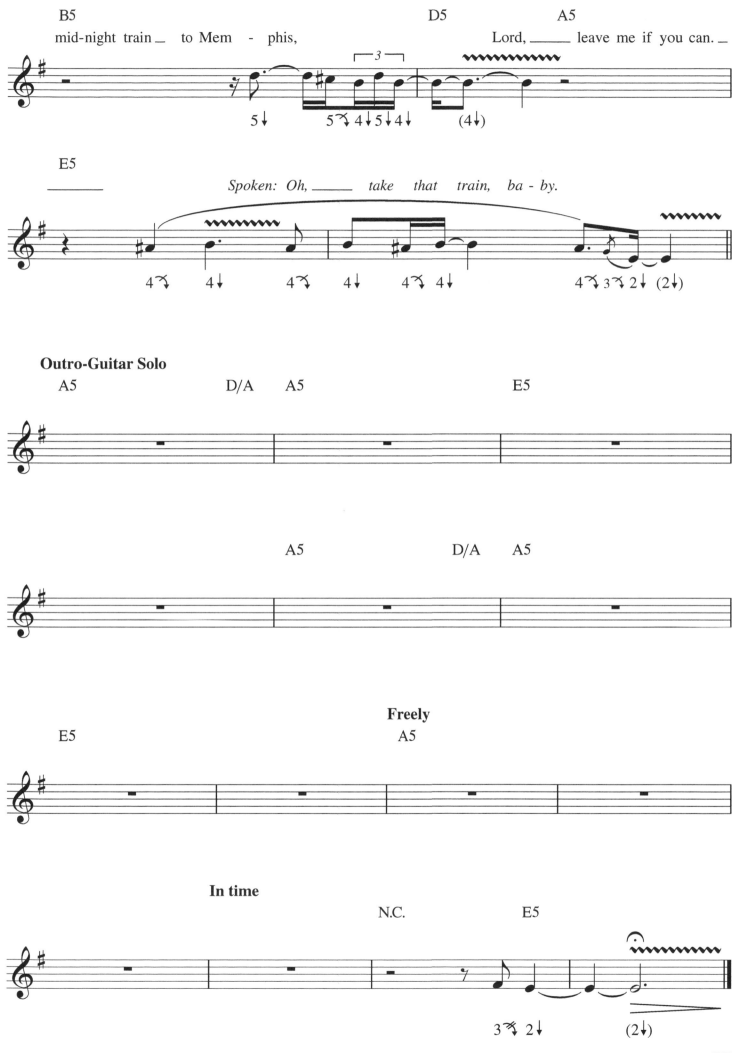

You Shook Me

Written by Willie Dixon and J.B. Lenoir

HARMONICA

Player: Robert Plant
Harp Key: A Diatonic

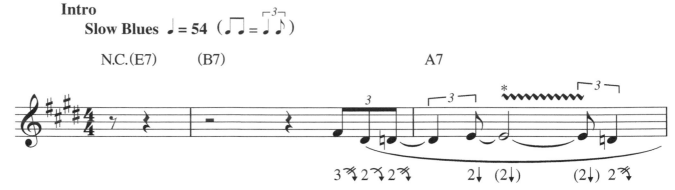

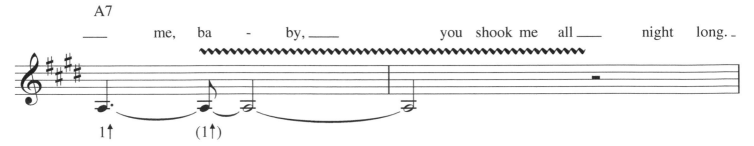

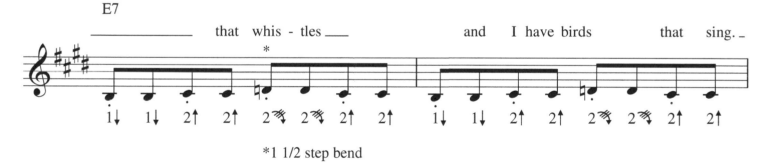

Verse

*1 1/2 step bend

59

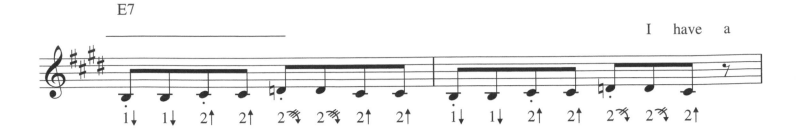

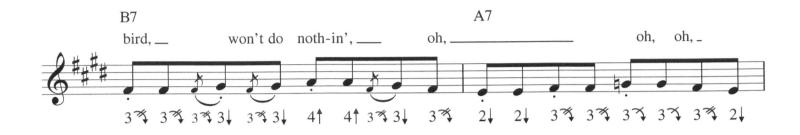

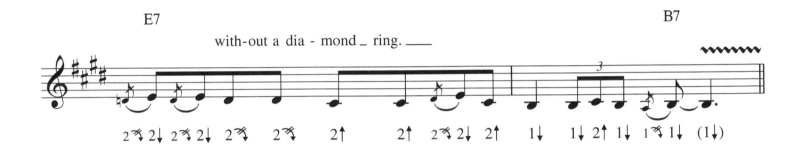

Organ Solo

Harmonica Solo

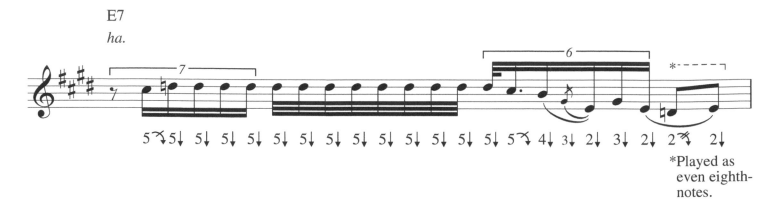

*Played as
even eighth-
notes.

*Wah-wah syllables.

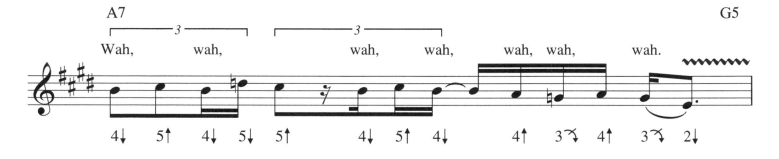

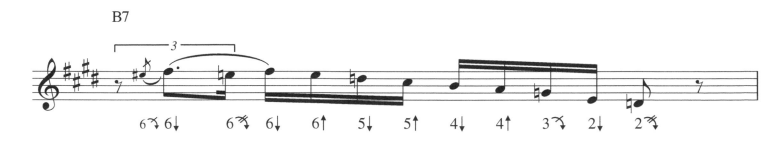

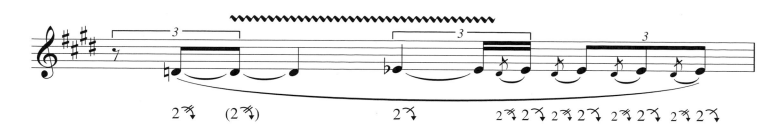

A7

E7

Wah,

Guitar Solo

E7   A7 N.C.   A7 N.C.   E7

Ha. _

B7   A7   E7   B7

3. You _ know you

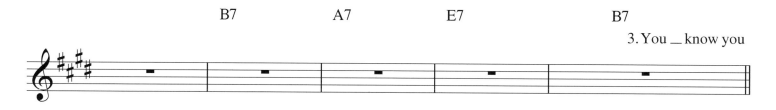

Verse

E7

shook me, babe, _   you shook me all ___ night long. _

I know you real-ly, real-ly did, babe. I think you shook _

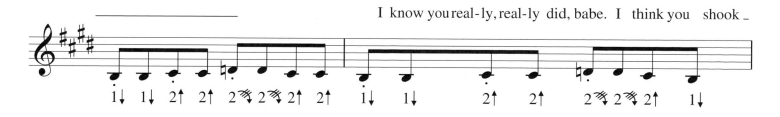